This Color and Cut Book Belongs To:

COLOR CUT AND GLUE

COLOR

1

CUT OUT

2

GLUE

3

USE EXAMPLE
In the corner of
each page or
YOUR IMAGINATION

Sometimes extra shapes are
included in case of accidents
or to make the picture your
way

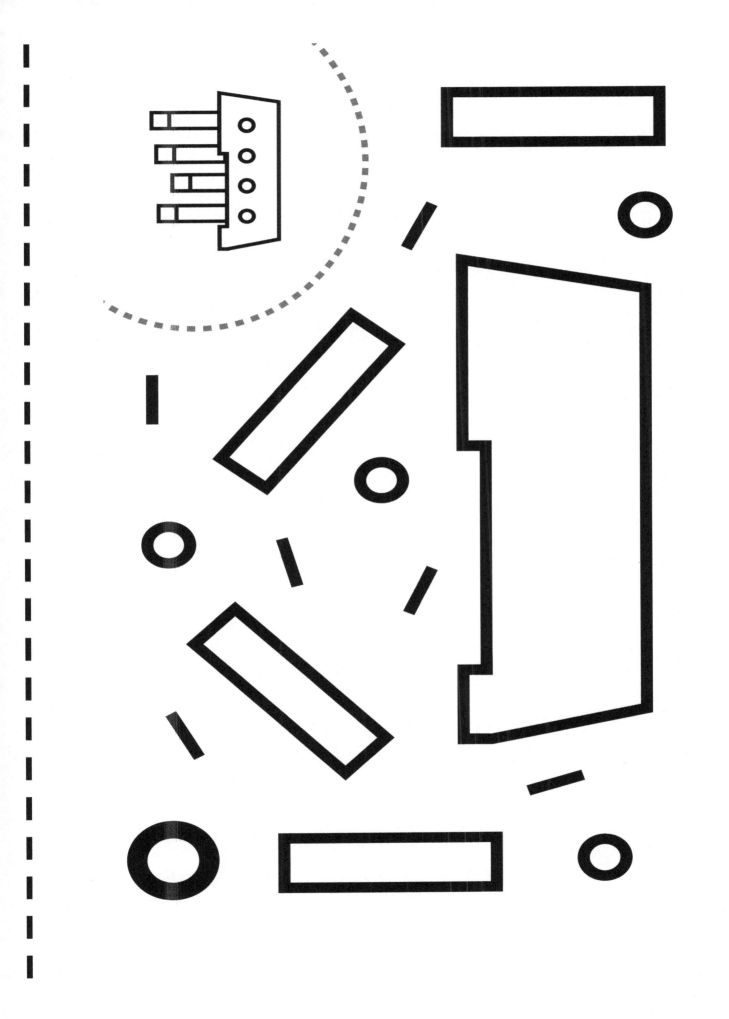

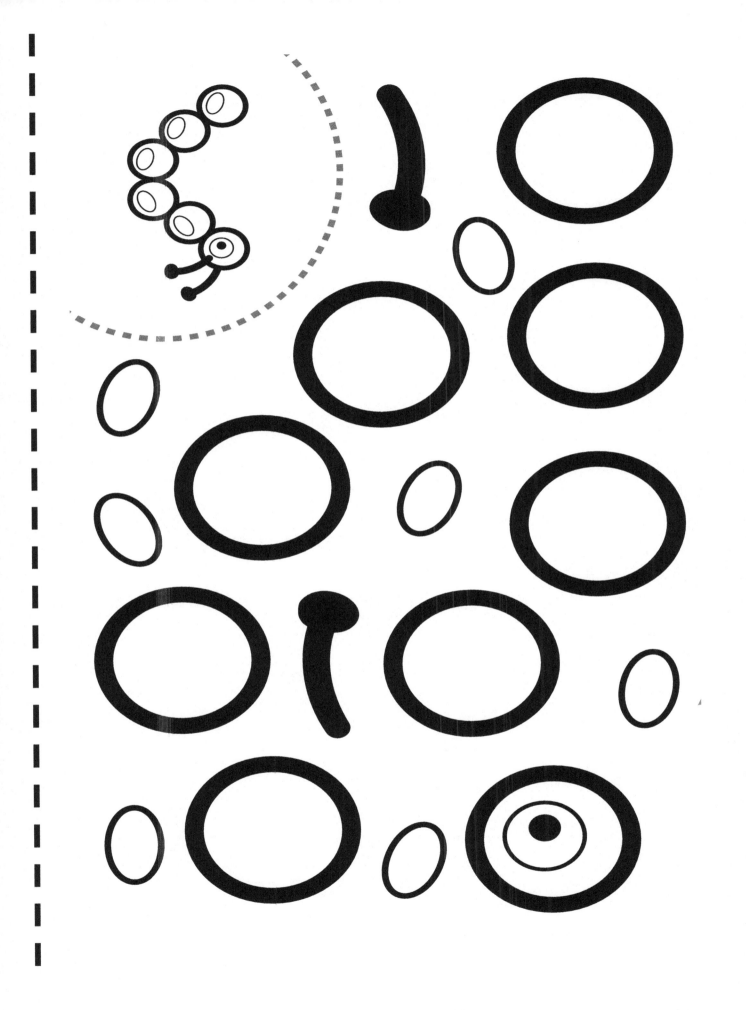

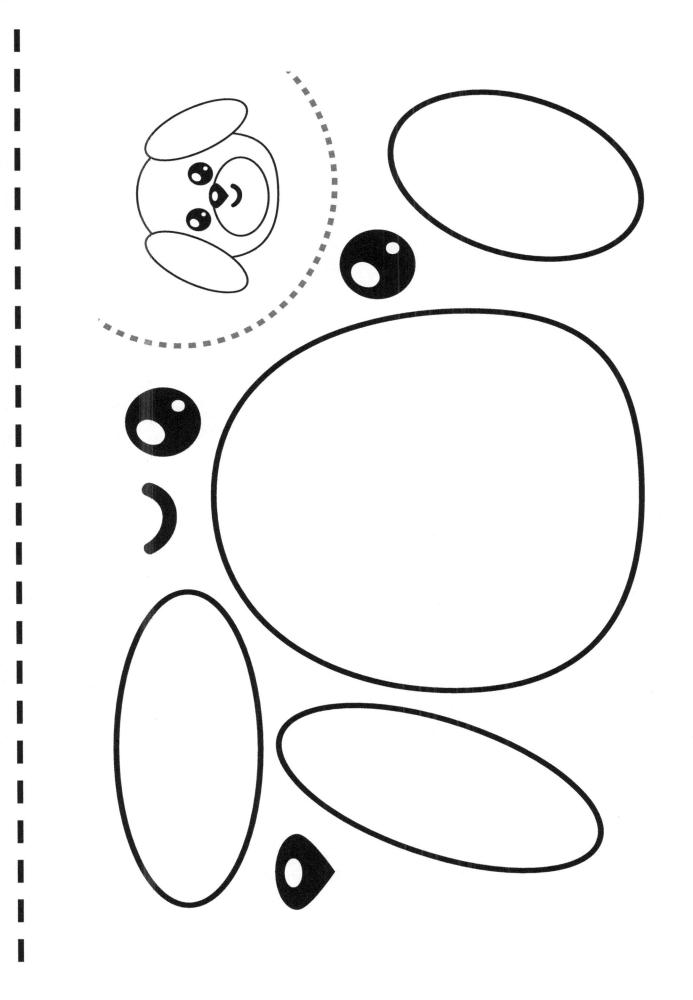

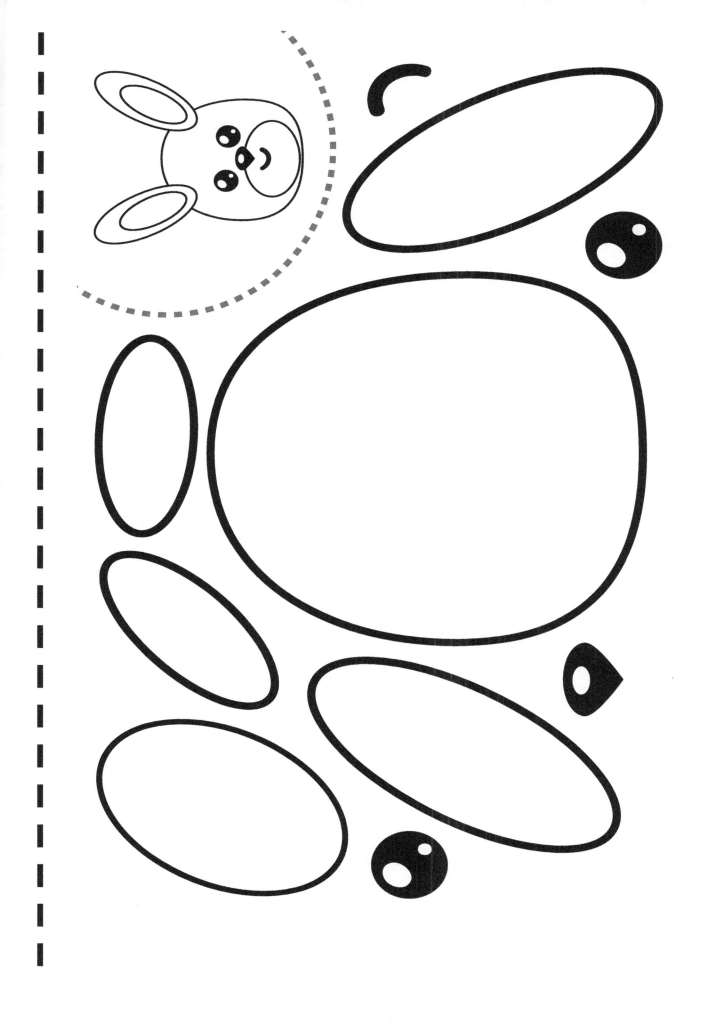

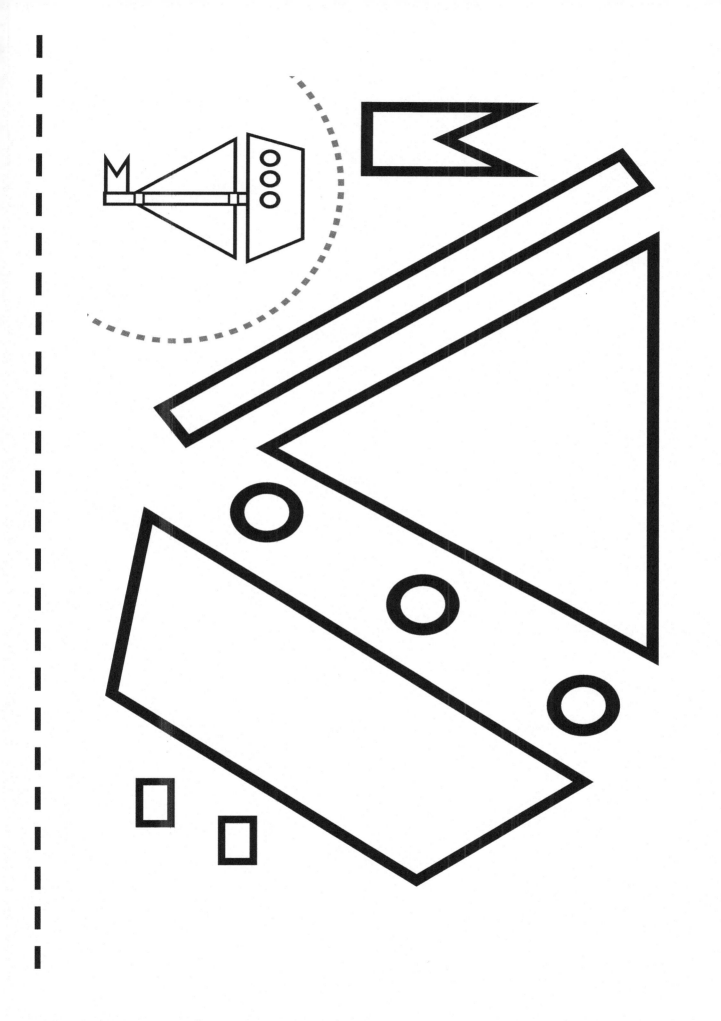

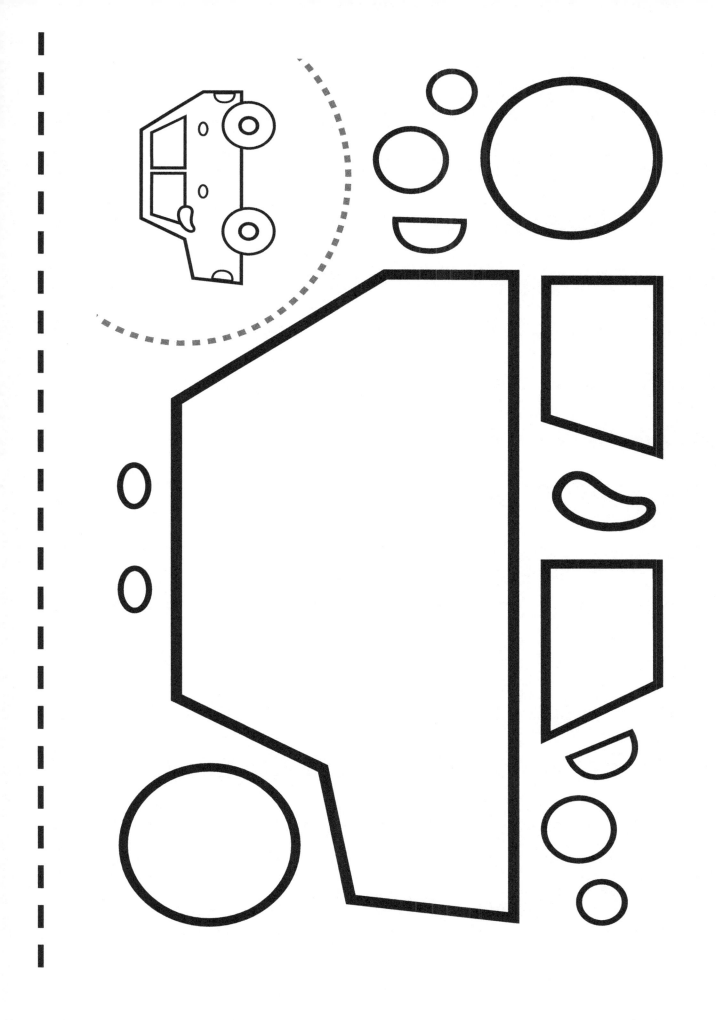

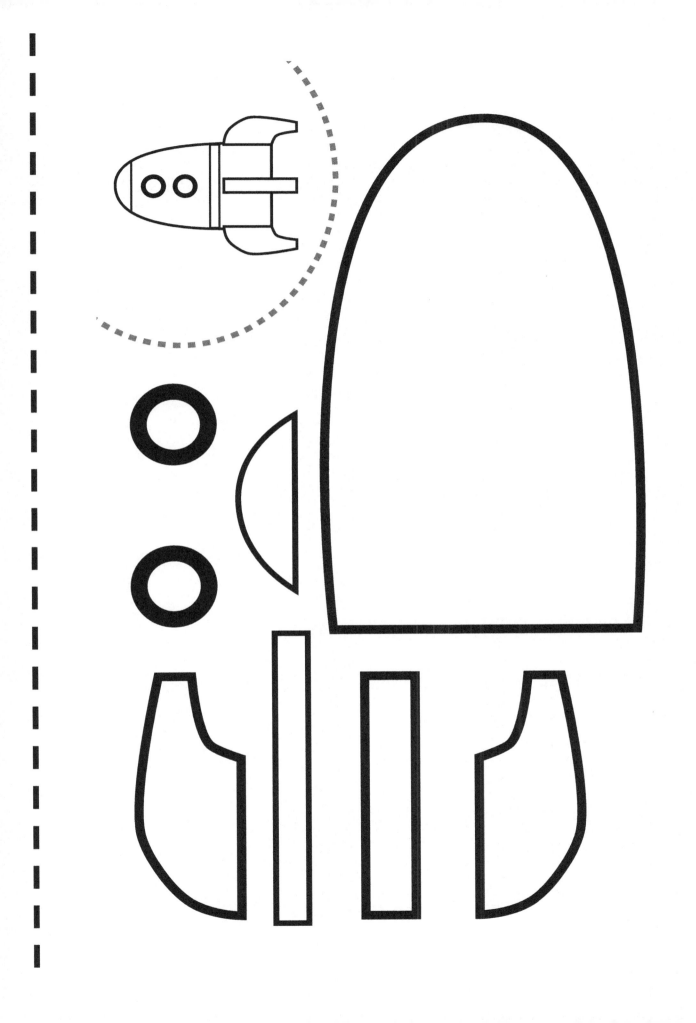

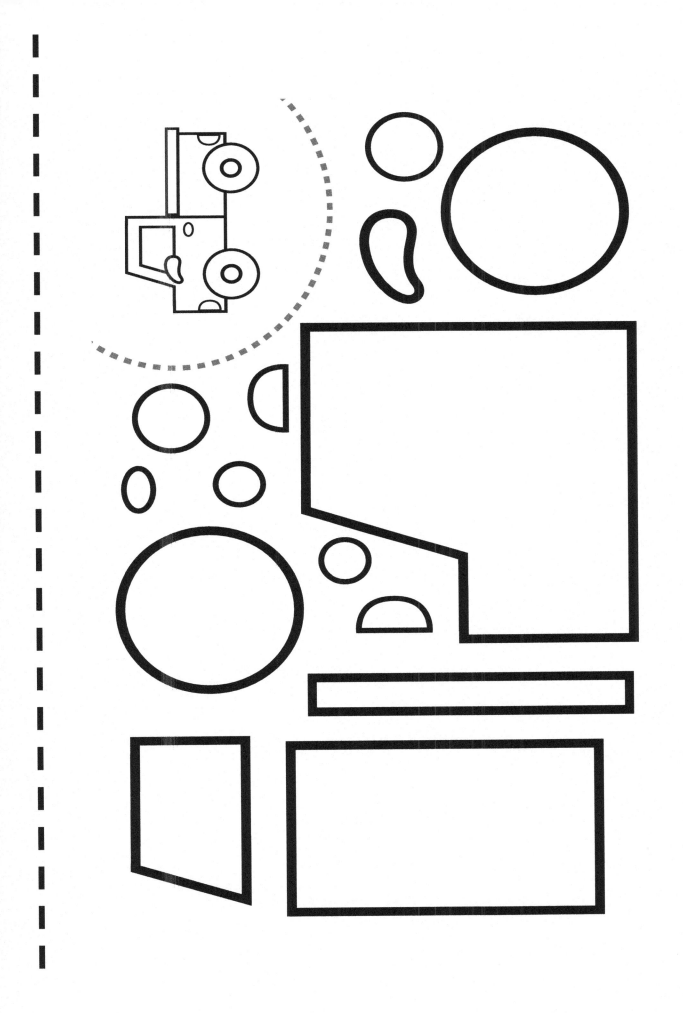

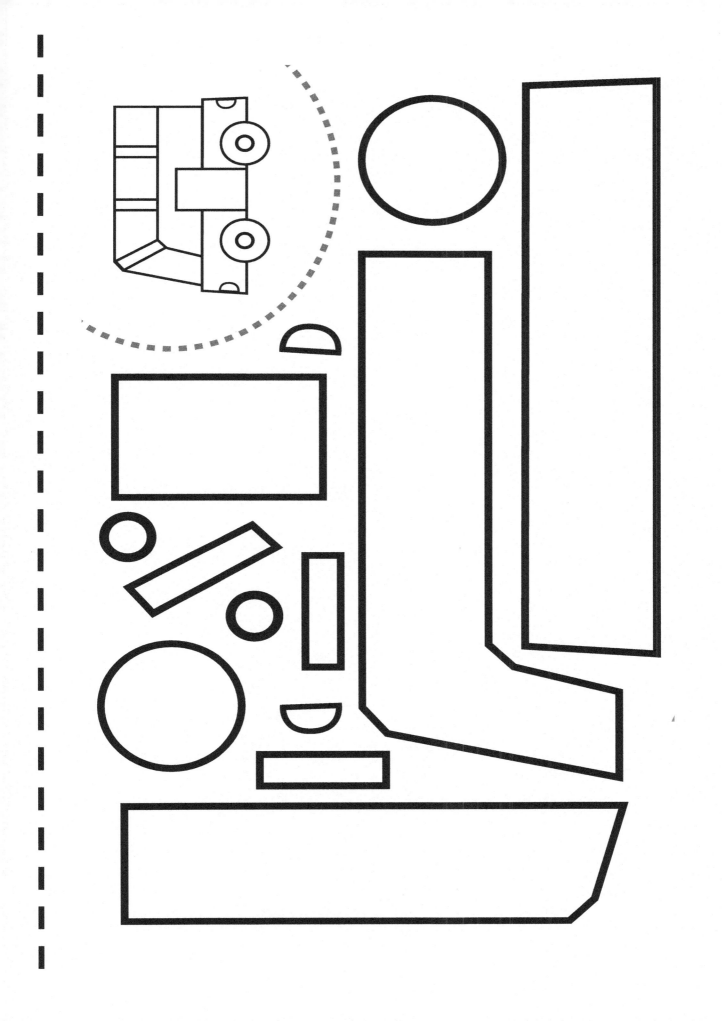

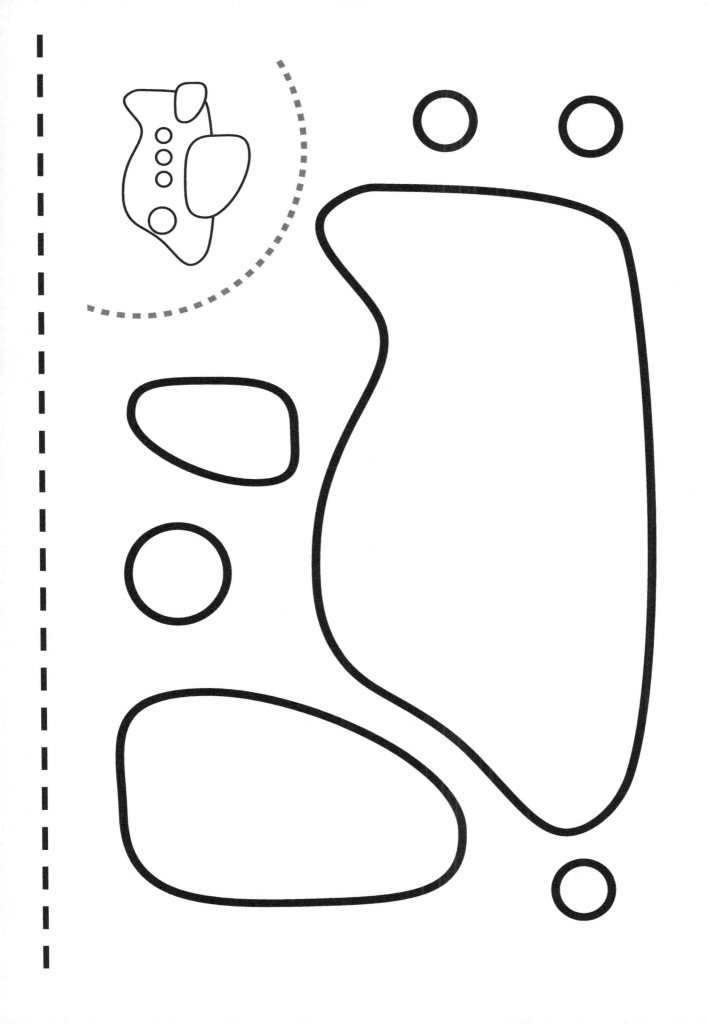

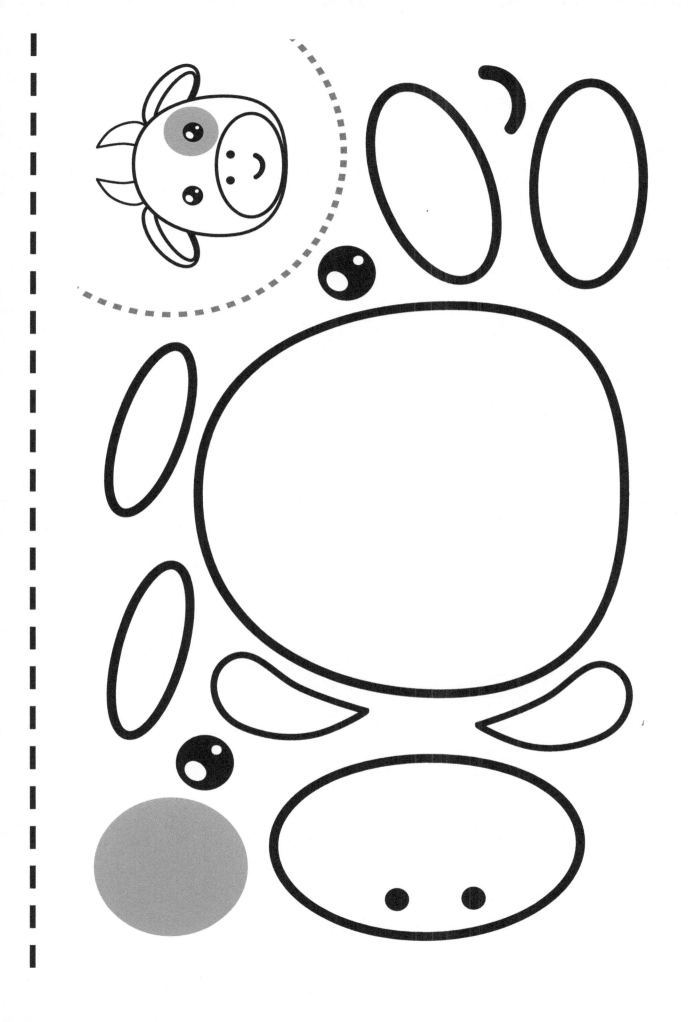

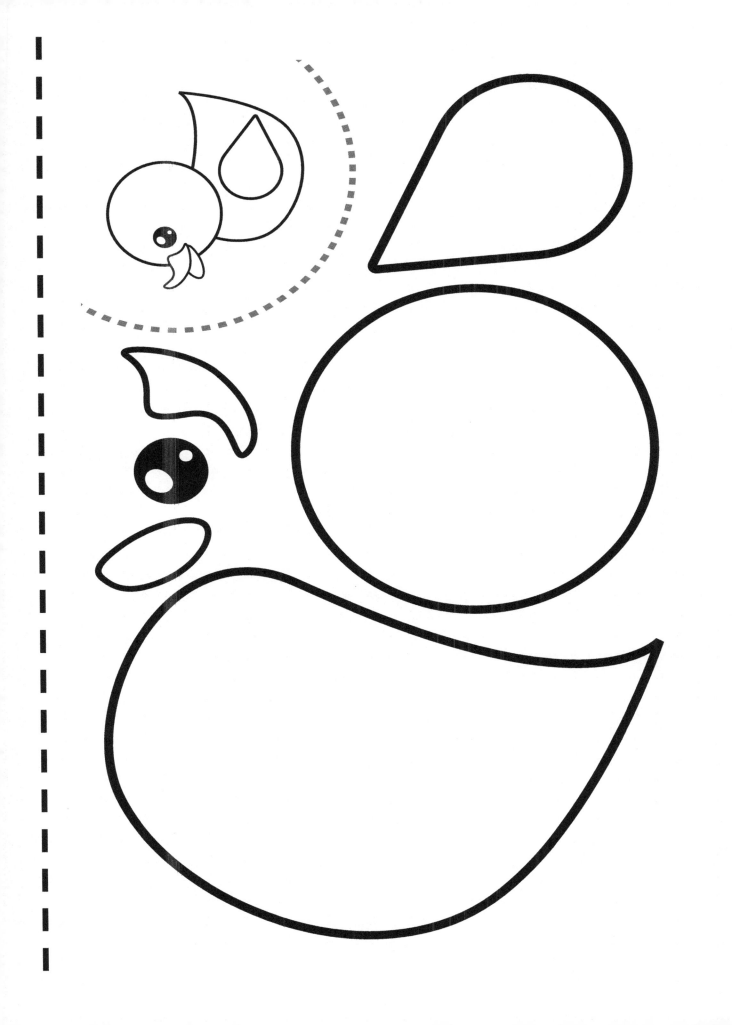

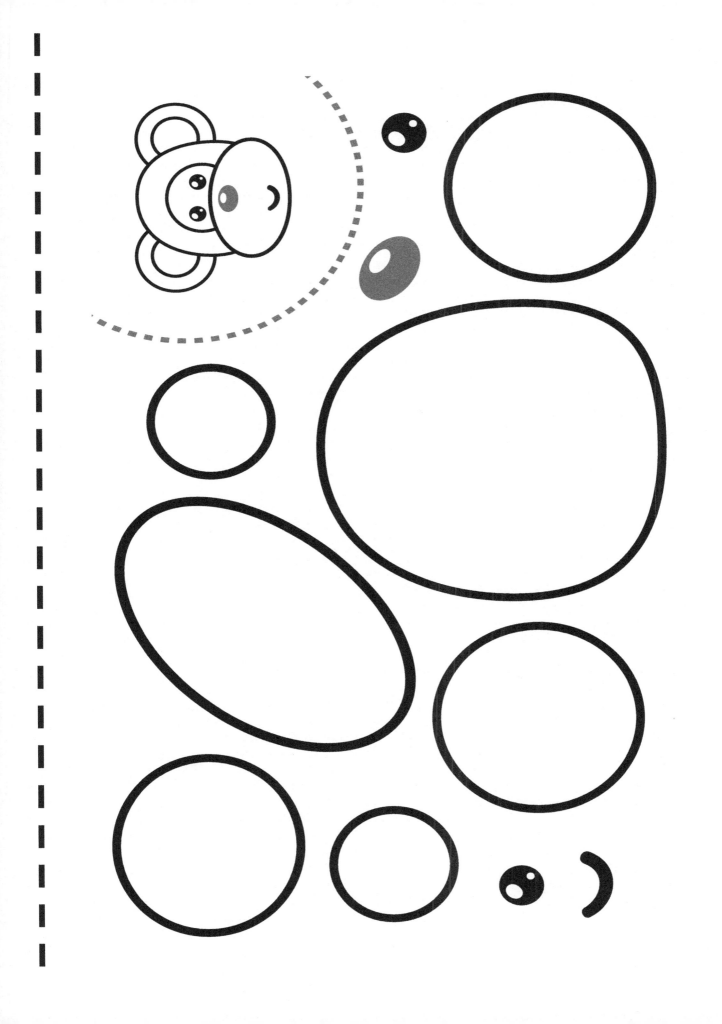

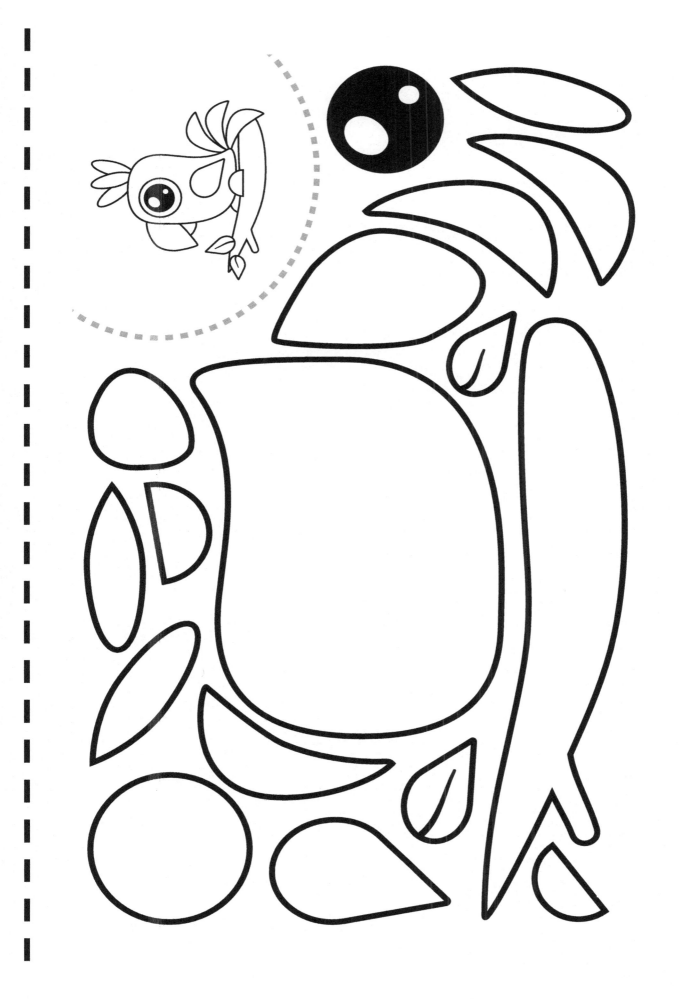

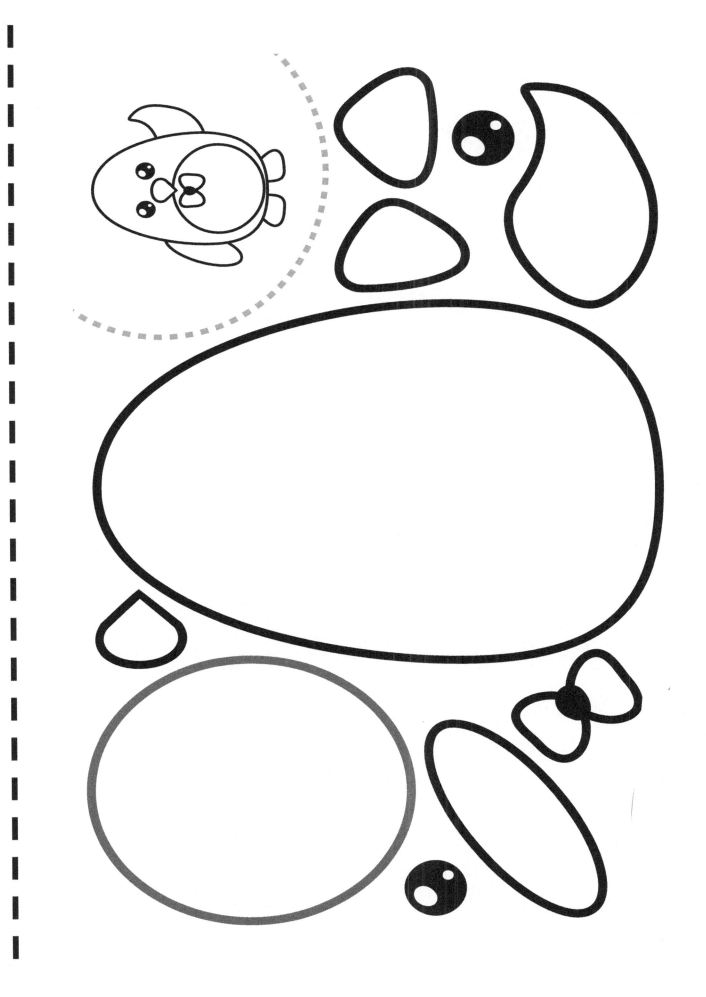

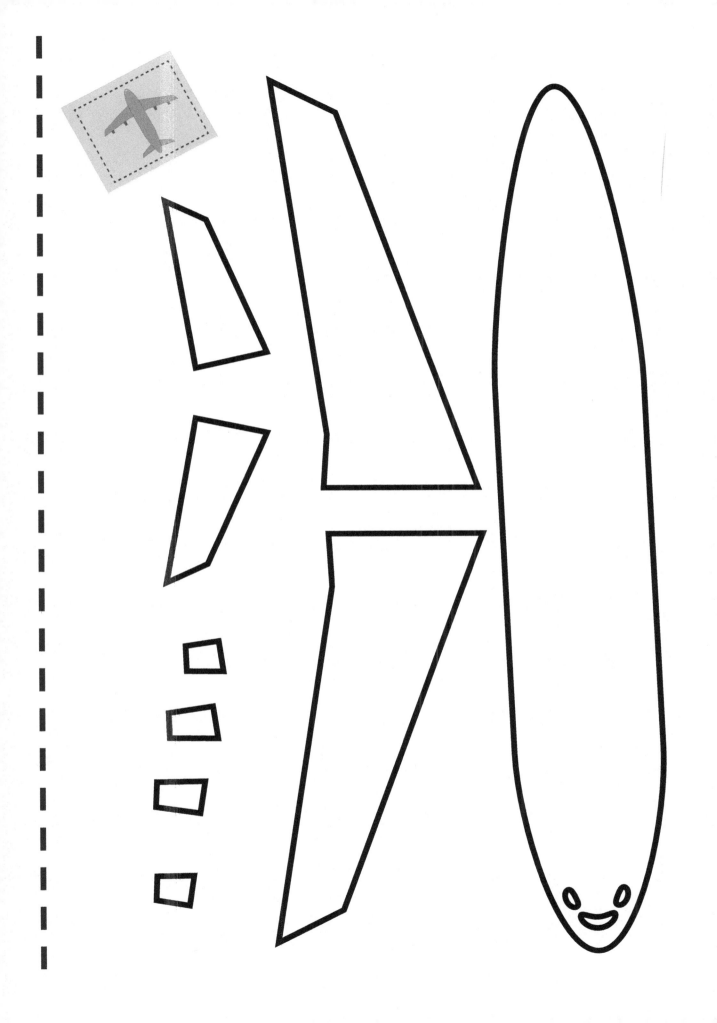

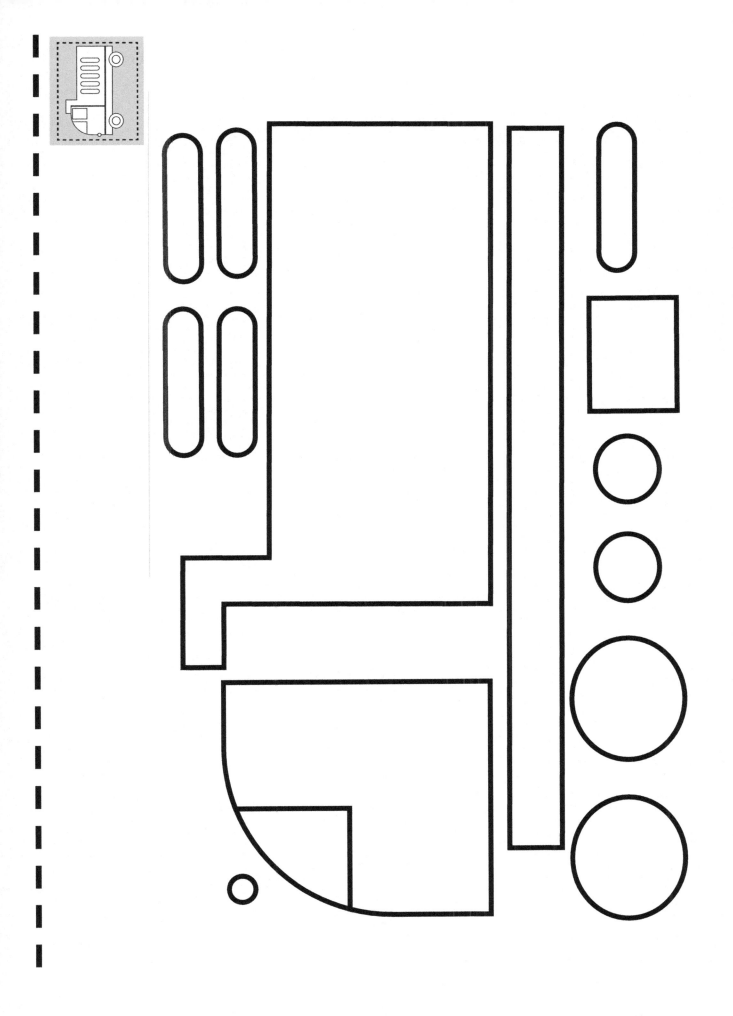

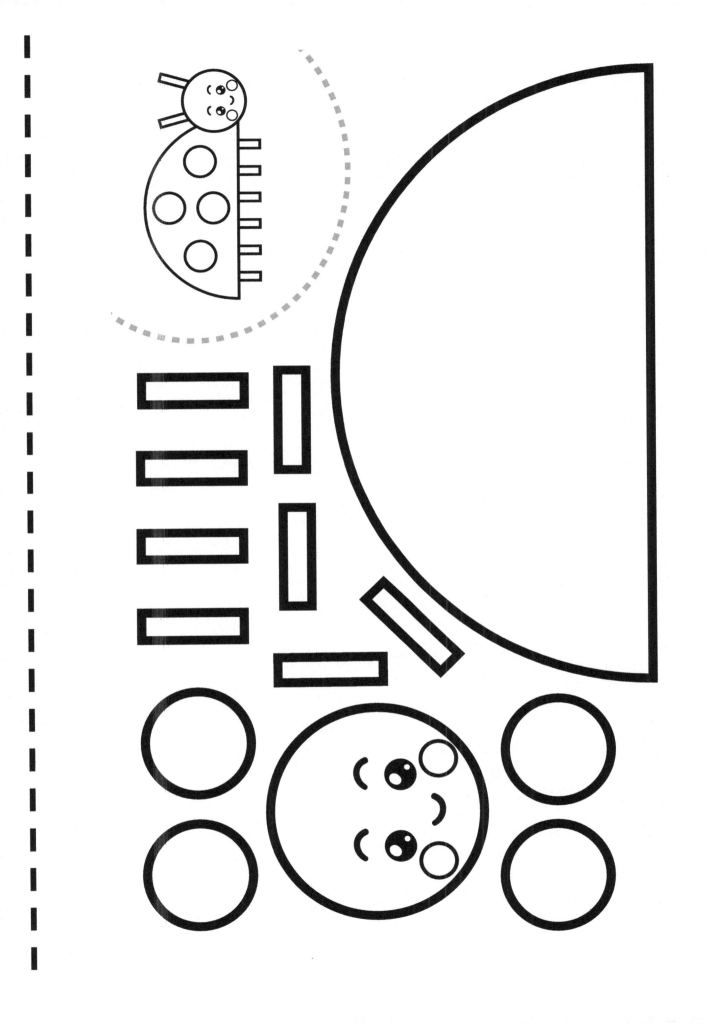

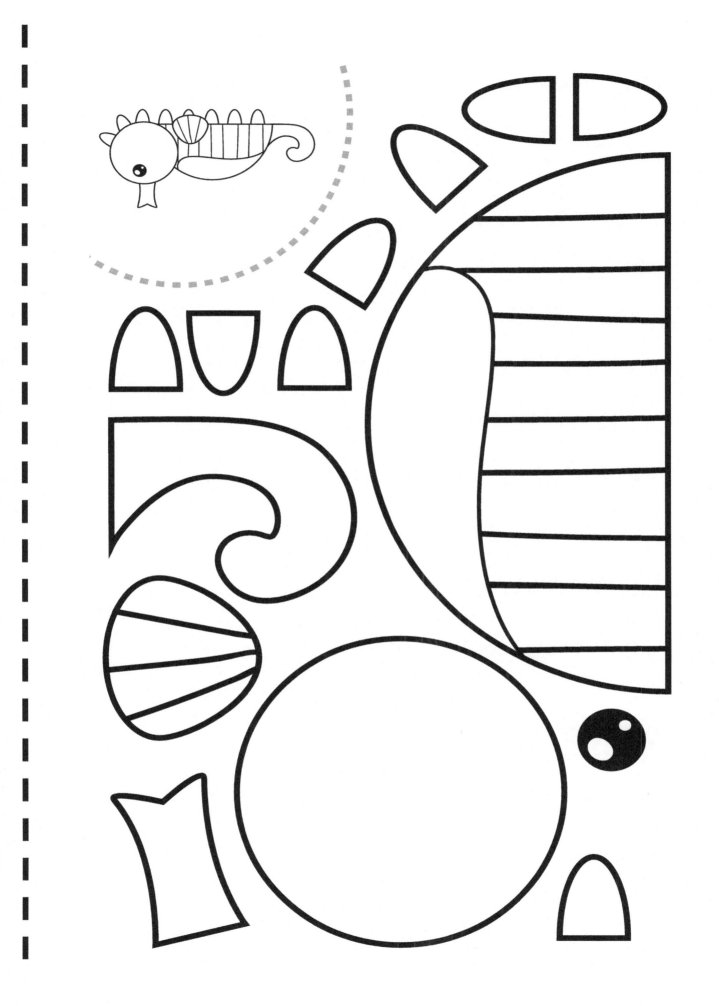

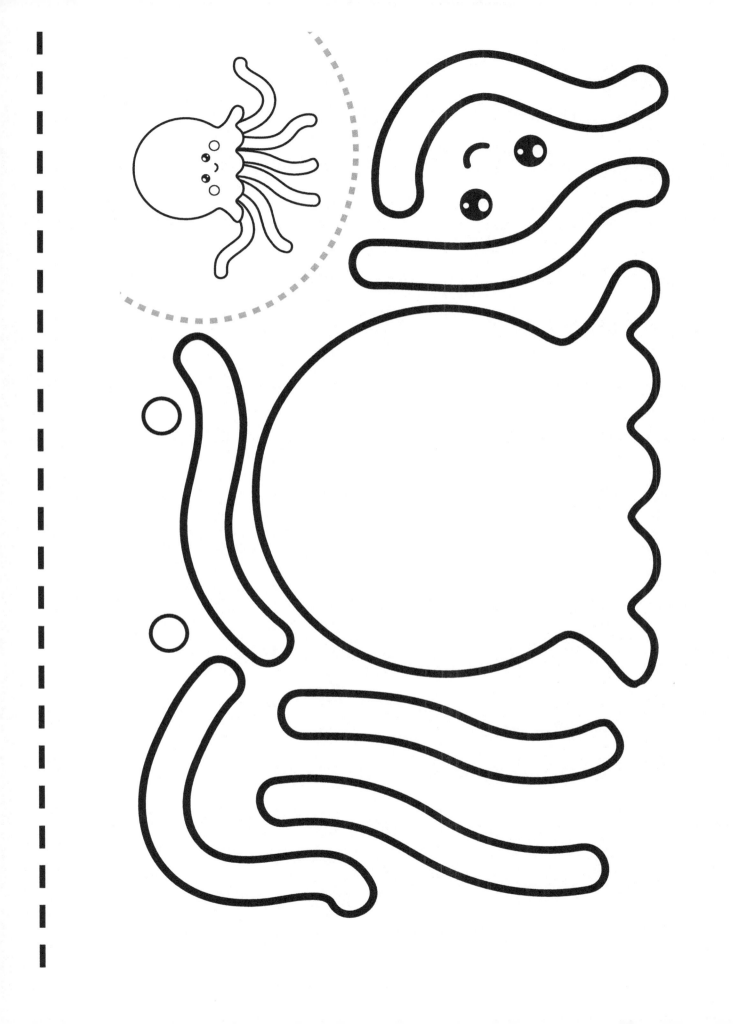

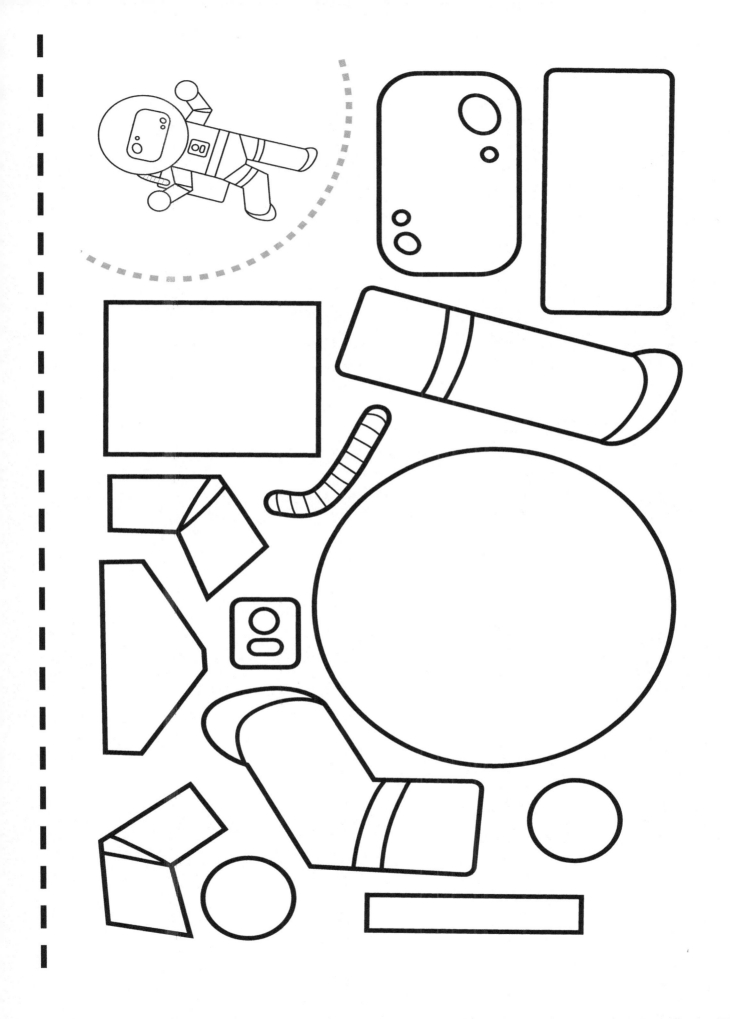

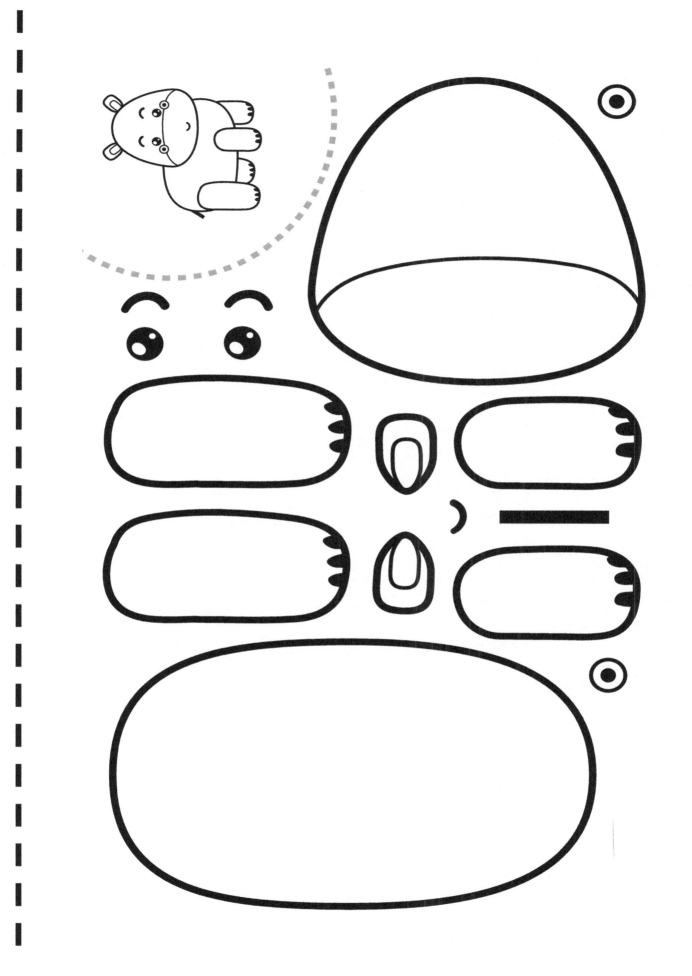

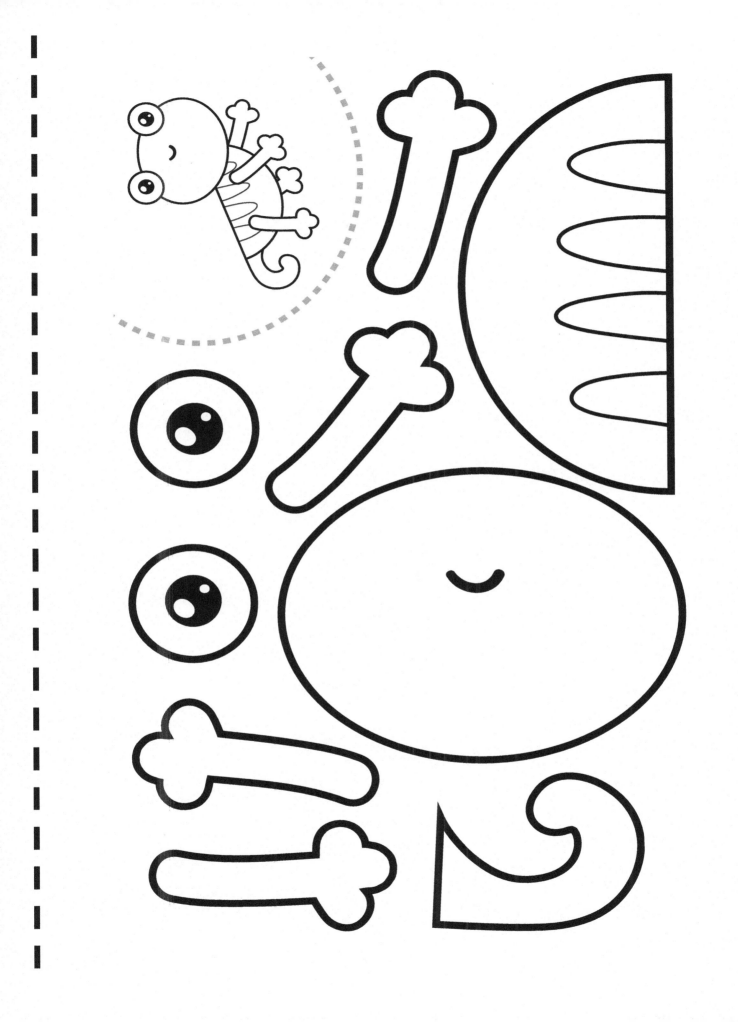

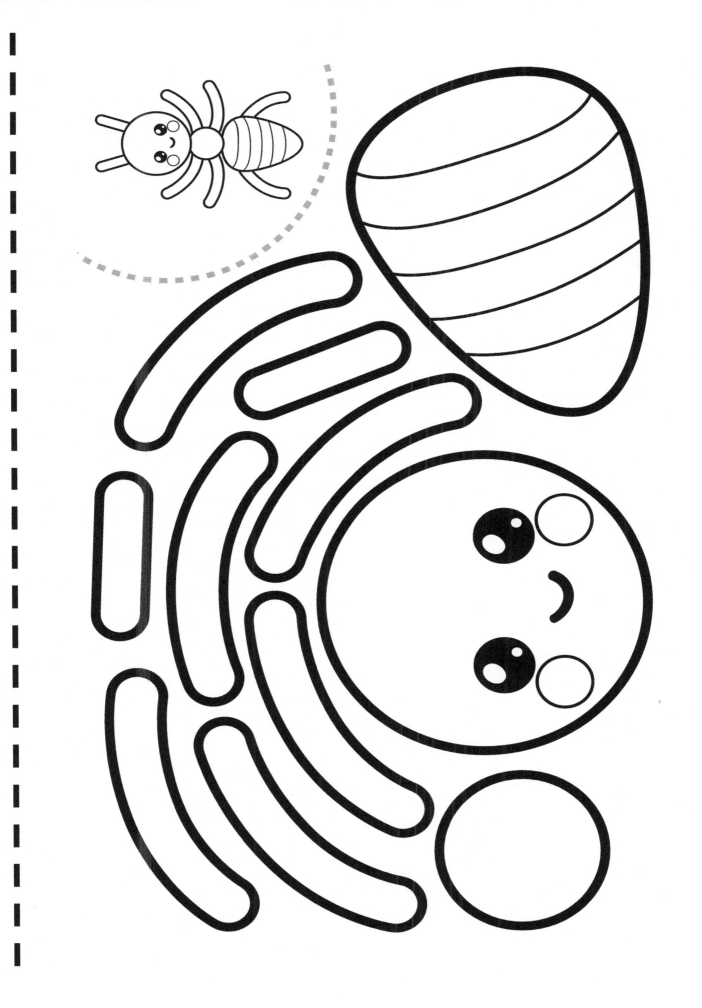

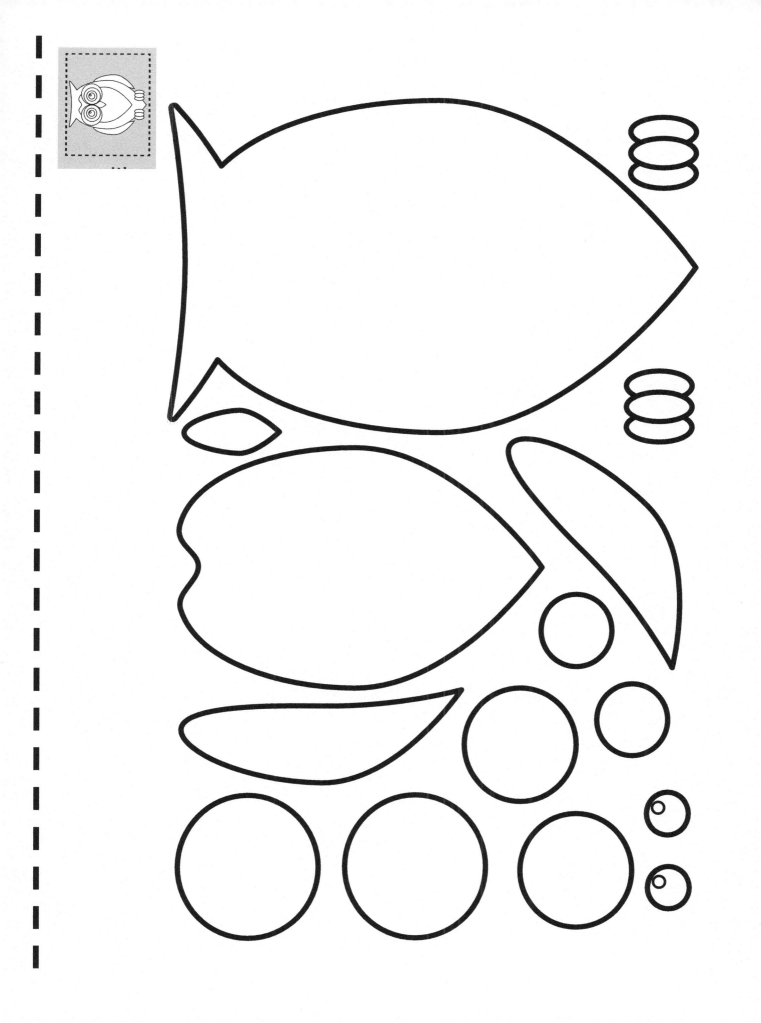

Made in the USA
Las Vegas, NV
14 December 2021